THE STAR-SPANGLED BANNER
★ CHARTS & TRACKS FOR S
Lead Sheets and Pro Backing Tracks in Various Keys & Styles

	PAGE	CD TRACK
ACOUSTIC GUITAR		
high key (B♭)	2	1
low key (G)	2	2
CONCERT BAND		
high key (B♭)	5	3
low key (A♭)	6	4
COUNTRY SHUFFLE		
high key (B♭)	5	5
low key (G)	7	6
GRAND PIANO		
high key (B♭)	8	7
low key (A♭)	10	8
JAZZ PIANO		
high key (B♭)	5	9
low key (G)	7	10
R&B (Modern)		
high key (B♭)	12	11
low key (G)	13	12
R&B (Traditional)		
high key (B♭)	5	13
low key (G)	7	14
STRING QUARTET		
high key (C)	14	15
low key (A)	15	16

ISBN 978-1-4803-2814-3

HAL•LEONARD®
CORPORATION

7777 W. BLUEMOUND RD. P.O. BOX 13819 MILWAUKEE, WI 53213

Visit Hal Leonard Online at
www.halleonard.com

THE STAR-SPANGLED BANNER

Words by FRANCIS SCOTT KEY
Music by JOHN STAFFORD SMITH

Capo III

With pride

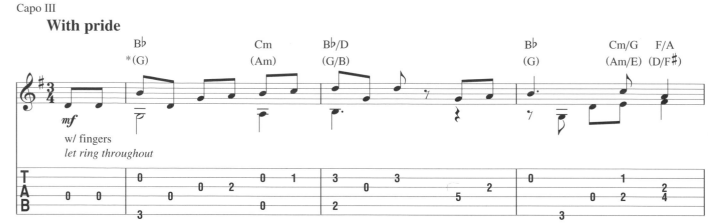

*Symbols in parentheses represent chord names respective to capoed guitar.
Symbols above reflect actual sounding chords. Capoed fret is "0" in tab.

Pitch: D
**4th string only

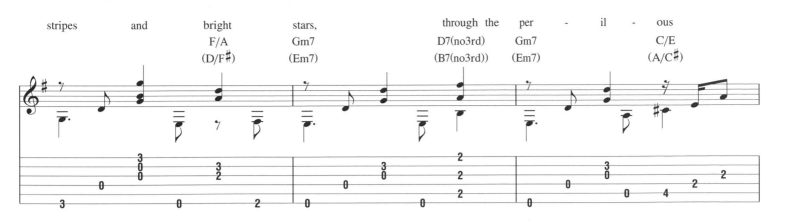

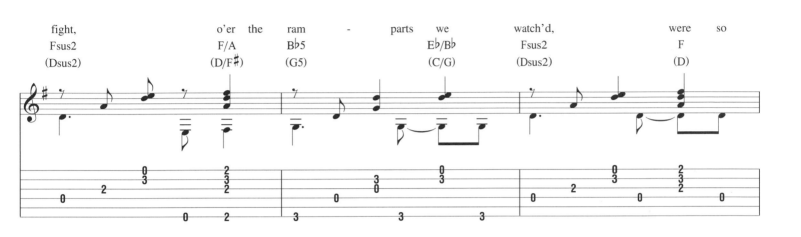

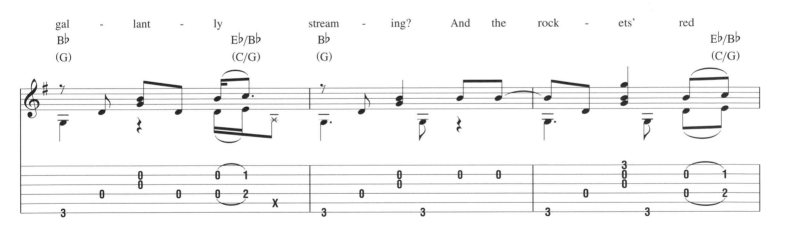

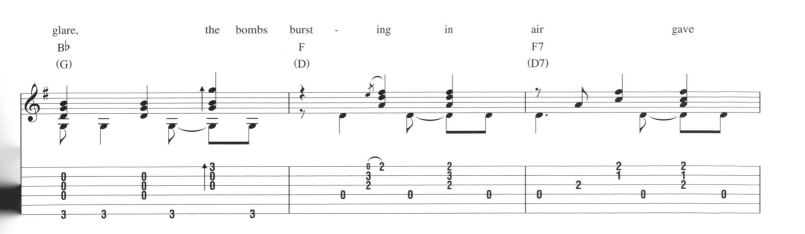

*Slap muted strings w/ picking hand.

THE STAR-SPANGLED BANNER

Words by FRANCIS SCOTT KEY
Music by JOHN STAFFORD SMITH

THE STAR-SPANGLED BANNER

Words by FRANCIS SCOTT KEY
Music by JOHN STAFFORD SMITH

With pride

THE STAR-SPANGLED BANNER

Words by FRANCIS SCOTT KEY
Music by JOHN STAFFORD SMITH

With pride

THE STAR-SPANGLED BANNER

Words by FRANCIS SCOTT KEY
Music by JOHN STAFFORD SMITH

With pride

O _____

say, can you see, by the dawn's ear - ly light, what so
stripes and bright stars, through the per - il - ous fight, what o'er the

proud - ly we hail'd, at the twi - light's last gleam - ing? Whose broad
ram - parts we watch'd, were so gal - lant - ly

THE STAR-SPANGLED BANNER

Words by FRANCIS SCOTT KEY
Music by JOHN STAFFORD SMITH

With pride

say, can you see, by the dawn's ear - ly light, what so
stripes and bright stars, through the per - il - ous fight, what o'er the

proud - ly we hail'd at the twi - light's last gleam - ing? Whose broad
ram - parts we watch'd, were so gal - lant - ly

THE STAR-SPANGLED BANNER

Words by FRANCIS SCOTT KEY
Music by JOHN STAFFORD SMITH

THE STAR-SPANGLED BANNER

Words by FRANCIS SCOTT KEY
Music by JOHN STAFFORD SMITH

THE STAR-SPANGLED BANNER

Words by FRANCIS SCOTT KEY
Music by JOHN STAFFORD SMITH

THE STAR-SPANGLED BANNER

Words by FRANCIS SCOTT KEY
Music by JOHN STAFFORD SMITH

With pride

O say, can you see, by the dawn's early light,
What so proudly we hailed at the twilight's last gleaming?
Whose broad stripes and bright stars, through the perilous fight,
O'er the ramparts we watched, were so gallantly streaming?
And the rockets' red glare, the bombs bursting in air
Gave proof through the night that our flag was still there.
O say, does that star-spangled banner yet wave
O'er the land of the free and the home of the brave?

On the shore dimly seen through the mists of the deep,
Where the foe's haughty host in dread silence reposes,
What is that which the breeze, o'er the towering steep,
As it fitfully blows, half conceals, half discloses?
Now it catches the gleam of the morning's first beam,
In full glory reflected now shines in the stream:
'Tis the star-spangled banner, O long may it wave
O'er the land of the free and the home of the brave.

And where is that band who so vauntingly swore
That the havoc of war and the battle's confusion,
A home and a country, should leave us no more?
Their blood has washed out their foul footsteps' pollution.
No refuge could save the hireling and slave
From the terror of flight, or the gloom of the grave:
And the star-spangled banner in triumph doth wave
O'er the land of the free and the home of the brave.

O thus be it ever, when freemen shall stand
Between their loved home and the war's desolation.
Blessed with vict'ry and peace, may the heav'n-rescued land
Praise the Power that hath made and preserved us a nation!
Then conquer we must, when our cause it is just,
And this be our motto: "In God is our trust."
And the star-spangled banner in triumph shall wave
O'er the land of the free and the home of the brave.

–Francis Scott Key, 1814

ACOUSTIC GUITAR
Joe Brasch, guitar

CONCERT BAND
U.S. Army Bands Online

COUNTRY SHUFFLE
Brent Edstrom, piano
Dru Heller, drums
Eugene Jablonsky, bass
Chris Howie, pedal steel
  and acoustic guitars

GRAND PIANO
J. Mark Baker, piano

JAZZ PIANO
Brent Edstrom, piano
Dru Heller, drums
Eugene Jablonsky, bass

R&B (Modern)
Arranged and realized
  by Brent Edstrom

R&B (Traditional)
Brent Edstrom, keyboards & piano
Dru Heller, drums
Eugene Jablonsky, bass

STRING QUARTET
Ilana Setapen, violin I
Timothy Klabunde, violin 2
Nathan Hackett, viola
Scott Tisdel, cello